Stuart Woodward
&
Paul Woodward

Living in the Light of Truth

Life Applications of Scriptures and the Consequences of Ignoring Them.

Nukan Publications

Living In The Light Of Truth

(Life Applications of Scriptures and the Consequences of Ignoring Them.)

By Stuart Woodward & Paul Woodward

ISBN-13: 978-1545131046
ISBN-10: 154513104X

Publisher: **Nukan Publications**

First Printed: **2017**

Cover Design: Design2Impact.co.uk

Dedication

This book is dedicated to our parents Leslie and Freda Woodward. At the time of writing they are still trusting the Lord aged 95, despite tough circumstances.

We are blessed to be their children and have learnt more than can be quantified through their influence and prayers.

Acknowledgement

We want to acknowledge the wonderful and varied people in each of the churches we have served. Through them we have learned so much and grown in our faith.

Foreword

Here is a book which shines a path through the self-focused culture in which we, as Christians, live and especially for those who want to live it on God's terms. It comes from the heart of those who have been pastorally responsible for literally thousands of lives between them. From that wealth of experience comes realism and practical wisdom about coping with the complexities of everyday Christian living which can be so easily dictated to by the worldly culture in which we live.

Here is a book which lays down essential, clear truths in a simple but profound way and which gives us a foundation upon which to evaluate our behaviour and attitudes toward the 'truths' that others (and sometimes ourselves) subtly demand that we submit ourselves to. It tackles, head on, the core issues that we live with today but only that we may know more of the wonder of God this side of heaven.

David Partington
Former Centre Director of Yeldall Manor
(A Christian drug addict rehab centre)
Former General Secretary of ISAAC (International Substance Abuse and Addiction Coalition)

Table of Contents

Introduction

This book emerged from both of us, independently, being provoked by God to make clear the need for people to make right choices as every choice brings consequences that can build or destroy. This is true for Christians and non-Christians alike. Our purpose is not primarily to defend or argue the point about biblical teaching on various subjects, though occasionally a little of this will be needed, but to outline and summarise some aspects of what the bible teaches regarding the subjects concerned. Then we will seek to apply that teaching to the lives of ordinary people today and spell out the consequences of the choices they make in relation to that teaching. This will be done both from within the bible's teaching about human experience and drawing on at least fifty years of pastoral experience between us.

Where we live and have recently served, both in Essex and Teesside, there are many social problems. The percentage of young people who go on to university is lower than that of many other places and it is not uncommon to have four generations of the same family living within a short distance of each of other. In a number of cases all the individuals survive on state benefit. Many women have children from various fathers and often the man who now lives in the house with them is the biological father of none of them. In a few cases a man has been left to bring up children who are not his as the mother has decided she cannot, or does not wish, to cope.

The individuals that we are referring to are all reaping the consequences of choices that they or others have made. Those choices have sprung from their understanding of truth, though they would seldom express it that way. However, somewhere along the line many have come to the view that the right to be happy is more important than anything else. They have imbibed a commonly held 'truth' but have seldom thought through the underlying issues.

As Christian leaders we feel God is drawing us to look again at the full breadth of 'The Great Commission' which we read in **Matthew 28:18-20 "Then Jesus came to them and said, 'All authority in heaven and on earth has been given to me. Therefore go and make disciples of all nations, baptising them in the name of the Father and of the Son and of the Holy Spirit, and teaching them**

to obey everything I have commanded you. And surely I am with you always, to the very end of the age.'"

We believe that teaching new disciples to make right choices and learn to obey everything Jesus commanded needs to become an increasing priority in the church.

Within the church we have Christians who have made choices and come to regret them, only now beginning to realise how their wrong understanding of truth has influenced those choices. We also have many who have come to faith and have begun to live a clearly Christian lifestyle whilst having to cope with the damage and heartache that remains from choices made before coming to faith.

Jesus said, '**you will know the truth and the truth will set you free' (John 8:32)**. He is the truth **(John 14:6)**. He is the word made flesh, and we MUST give ourselves over to what Jesus reveals to us in scripture about:

- God
- Humanity
- The Cross
- The Church
- Money

- Sex
- etc.

At the end of what is commonly known as the Sermon on the Mount Jesus presents us with a stark alternative. In **Matthew 7:24-27** He very clearly says: **'Everyone who hears these words of mine and puts them into practice'** is like the wise one whose house is securely founded and survives the storm. Alternatively He says: **'Everyone who hears these words of mine and does not put them into practice'** is like the foolish one whose house is insecure and collapses in adverse conditions.

Even a very superficial reading of **John 17** makes it clear that truth is the basis on which Christians can know unity. There can be no real unity without it. The western world is well on the way to emerging fully out of the existential foolishness of the latter part of the twentieth century. Statements like, 'that may be true for you but it is not for me' and 'that may be your truth but it is not mine' are becoming rarer as the movers and shakers of the day realise a world without absolutes is impossible. Sadly this is leading into a new form of absolutism, of which most are blissfully unaware, where the values of secular humanism must not be challenged on pain of ridicule or much worse.

As soon as we compromise on truth, that is the truth of all the above and much more, we open ourselves up to self-reliance and demonic deception. The truth that is Jesus, revealed through God's word is our only hope.

Without it we can never be free.

It is not that we expect all who read this to agree with all we write. However, we do want to provoke thought and cause people to think through the consequences of how they respond to God and His revelation.

We want that the mind might be provoked and enlightened but also that this may in turn lead to the spirit being touched and sensitivity to God heightened.

Chapter 1

The Truth About God

'I find life quite simple really,' confided Bill. 'Whenever I have a problem I just have a word with my old mate upstairs and He sorts it out.'

'Isn't it wonderful that God loves me? He thinks I am the greatest thing imaginable and if He had a fridge He would have a fridge magnet with my name on it. I just know that however much I fail Him He just smiles and tells me not to be quite so silly next time.' These are Maisie's words of wisdom.

'I don't like to make a fuss,' said Fred, 'but you really must stop that young man wearing his baseball cap in church. It dishonours God.'

'I am afraid I might have to stop attending baptism

services,' said Gladys, 'because I cannot stand it when everyone bursts into applause when someone is baptised. We should not be clapping for them. We should be reverencing God.'

Comments like these are not uncommon. Amongst other things they reveal something of each speaker's understanding of God. It is probably fair to say that our understanding of what and who God is affects our understanding of every other area of life.

Truth.

How easy it is to call God 'Father' without really understanding what we are saying. Our temptation is to make God in our own image.

We can imagine God as some benevolent Father/Grandfather type with a long flowing white beard or we can imagine Him as the stern demanding Father who is always difficult to please. Neither is correct.

It is vital that our understanding and knowledge of God only comes from the revelation that He gives to us of Himself. He does that in a number ways.

The bible says: ***'The heavens declare the glory of God; the skies proclaim the work of His hands'.*** (Psalm 19:1)

Creation itself bears witness to His existence to such an extent that Paul is clear that no-one can have any excuse for not worshipping Him and depending on Him.

Romans 1:18-20 says ***'The wrath of God is being revealed from heaven against all the godlessness and wickedness of people, who suppress the truth by their wickedness, since what may be known about God is plain to them, because God has made it plain to them. For since the creation of the world God's invisible qualities – his eternal power and divine nature – have been clearly seen, being understood from what has been made, so that people are without excuse.'***

God has, at different times, revealed something of Himself to people through angelic visitations, theophanies (pre-incarnation appearances of the Son) and visions. He has revealed Himself very clearly through the scriptures of the Old and New Testaments.

The bible also makes it very clear that God had no beginning and will have no end. Before everything that we experience existed (and indeed all perceivable reality) there was God. He will never come to an end. He is totally self-sustaining. He needs nothing and is fully complete in Himself. There is nothing He does not know (*omniscience*), nowhere He is not present (*omnipresence*) and nothing beyond His power (*omnipotence*). Everything else that exists besides God He has created, or is a consequence of that creation. He is not limited in any way except when He chooses to limit Himself because He knows it is for the best. He is not the same as creation (*pantheism*) and is not in His creation (*panentheism*) except insofar as His creation can reveal His handiwork because it reveals something of Him, as a painting can express something of the nature of the artist.

The primary way God reveals Himself to us though is through Jesus.

Hebrews 1:3 tells us: ***'The Son is the radiance of God's glory and the exact representation of His being, sustaining all things by His powerful word'.***

Colossians 2:19 tells us: ***'For in Christ all the fullness of the Deity lives in bodily form'.***

Having revealed Himself most completely in the man Christ Jesus He then poured out His own Spirit upon those who believed in Him, writing His law on their hearts, and taking up residence at the centre of their lives. In this way He can be known not just objectively but subjectively, as His internal presence interacts with every aspect of our being and sets us apart for Him.

Although only one God, He has revealed Himself in three persons, Father, Son and Holy Spirit. Each of these persons exist together as one God, modelling perfect community and perfect harmony. Each person is equally omniscient, omnipresent and omnipotent. Each person is equally eternal. The Son continually proceeds from the Father and always has done. The Spirit continually applies the Father's purposes and always has done.

The partial exception to some of this was while the Son lived His life on earth. He chose to be limited and live dependently on the Holy Spirit in order to live a fully human life. As a child in the manger He did not think to Himself: 'I know everything but in order to keep the image I will cry and pretend ignorance'. He had to grow and learn. He did not exercise His earthly ministry until the Holy Spirit came upon Him. Of course there was authority in His name but the power was a derived one as He ministered in the power of the Spirit. The only functional difference between Him and us when He lived on this earth is that He was without sin.

God reveals Himself in scripture as a God of love, caring about His creation (even sparrows) and expressing compassion towards human beings. However, He is also revealed as a God who is holy, who hates and will not tolerate sin. He is a God of justice and judgement and all human beings will one day have to give account to Him. Unatoned for sin cannot be allowed in His holy presence and human beings will have a destiny of living in His presence eternally, often described as heaven, or living excluded from His experienced presence eternally, often described as hell. What is said about hell makes it clear that the experience of it will be dreadful and far worse than any human experience in this life.

Of course much more could be said about God but we have to stop somewhere. We will now turn our minds to the application of these truths to everyday living before looking at the consequences of the choices we make in the light of this application.

Application.

The first and most obvious thing that comes to mind is that reality and life's purpose has to centre in God, not in human desire or progress. Popular and almost unchallenged statements become rather exposed. Shakespeare's advice that we each should above all else 'to thine own self be true' becomes a rather foolish idea.

Making a statement about the conduct of our lives by choosing at our funeral Frank Sinatra singing 'I did it my way' moves from being admirable to tragic. He is God and to miss Him is to miss life's meaning and value. Perhaps that is why the Psalmist tells us that it is the fool who says in His heart there is no God.

In Isaiah 9:6 we read: ***'For to us a child is born, to us a son is given, and the government will be on his shoulders. And he will be called Wonderful Counsellor, Mighty God, Everlasting Father, Prince of Peace.'***

So God is the Everlasting Father. Our question then is what is the everlasting Father like and how do we relate to Him?

Because Christians are hidden in Christ, God the Father wants us to have the same relationship with Him that Jesus has i.e. a relationship of sonship, dependency, intimacy and accountability.

We have no personal relationship with the Father other than through Jesus. Now that we are in Christ we can know the joy and freedom of being a child of God.

A life lived without the centrality of God as our Father, whether that life is wasted on drugs and self-pleasure or 'usefully spent' in humanly more praiseworthy pastimes, is a life that has missed the whole point of existence.

God has revealed Himself completely in Jesus Christ and so He must be centre stage when we consider how human life should be lived. To ignore His teaching and the salvation He offers through His death and resurrection puts us in the position of the man who built His house on the sand. To seek to live by His teaching and avail ourselves of so great a salvation puts us in the position of the man who built His house on the rock. Failure to live as those who are accountable can only lead to disaster.

God's existence as one but three stresses the great importance of community and speaks volumes regarding what God wants for human beings and in particular for how God wants His church to conduct itself. We are called to model a different way of living, one of mutual service and perfect love.

The triune nature of God also has implications for how we regard ourselves as human beings, for the bible tells us human beings are uniquely made in the image of God (more on this later). That being the case, His triune nature must be reflected in us and, we believe, testifies to each human being composed of body, soul and spirit.

God as holy and pure sends us a clear message that sin is serious. Our sin is not a little problem that God smilingly overlooks. It, in all its forms, offends God, effectively spits in His face, separates us from God and if left unattended dooms us for eternity.

For those who have repented and put their trust in Jesus Christ the truth about God reminds us that as human beings life is to be lived in the power of the Holy Spirit. Jesus modelled this for us and the same Holy Spirit who rested and remained on Him at His baptism is the one who indwells us and under whose leadership and guidance we are to live our lives.

When God is understood in this way we come to realise that He alone is the arbiter of what is good and what is not. He has total rights over all creation and is being right and good when He has mercy on whom He chooses to have mercy. **Romans 9:1-28** carries Paul's coherent but unpopular perspective that God is the potter. The clay has no right to complain. ***'But who are you, O man, to talk back to God?'*** (Romans 9:20).

In summary the truth about God is not to be considered in the abstract but has vital and practical applications to the basis on which we choose to live our lives. To say God is holy and to minimise the gravity of sin is a contradiction. To believe that He is the eternal Creator and Judge and still insist on living lives our own way means that such belief is mere lip service. To claim to believe that Jesus is the perfect revelation of God and be selective about which parts of His teaching we accept is to prove that we do not believe it at all.

Consequences

There are huge consequences either way in getting a right understanding about God. A right understanding of God is essential if we are not to drift into untold error.

God is our Father through our response to and relationship with Jesus the Son and so we are filled and empowered by the Holy Spirit to enable us effectively to live as children of God.

Living this way enables us to:

- Live in our new identity as children of God
- Be filled with the Holy Spirit on a continual basis
- Enjoy the word as it lights our way
- Hear the Fathers voice
- Enjoy the adventure of faith

A faulty understanding of who God is or a failure to seriously apply a right understanding also brings consequences. Those who choose not to believe in God have to find another outlet for their worship instinct. Thus for some, humanity is the ultimate reality and all have to serve human development. For others it is 'mother earth' who demands our all-consuming attention. Other worship objects can be riches, family, career and so on. Mark Driscoll has frequently pointed out that you can usually tell what a person worships when you ask what they think about most, what occupies most of their time and what they spend most of their money on.

For those who claim to believe in God, many of the same problems apply. Many who claim to be Christians are still besotted by self-fulfilment, happiness and the like. The Christian young adult who chooses sexual relationships outside the concept of life long union will tell us that they know it is not God's best way but as it makes them happy it must be OK. The 'if it feels good it must be good' philosophy of life is astonishingly common. Subtly many have come to believe in a god whose purpose is to meet their need and scratch where they itch. Tough times come and God, who clearly doesn't do His job properly, is jettisoned or relegated to the fringes of life. The parable of the sower swiftly comes to mind!

In years of ministry we have known quite a few praising and prominent church folk drift away when God didn't stop them being made redundant or stop some other hardship from entering their lives. In fairness some preachers and teachers share the blame for this in implying by their teaching that God exists to make us happy forgetting that Jesus told us it is when we seek first the Kingdom and His righteousness that the other stuff takes care of itself.

The Pharisees had narrowed down true reverence to a lengthy set of rules. Jesus took pleasure in breaking some. The healing of a man on the Sabbath, the picking of ears of corn on the Sabbath, not bothering with ceremonial hand washing and speaking to a Samaritan woman whilst alone are just some examples. Our view of

God determines our choices and our choices bring consequences. We can worry about a baseball cap or applause at a baptism service, forgetting to ask what is in the heart of those involved. We can see God as our benevolent Uncle or Pal upstairs and fail to recognise that He is a consuming fire and an eternal judge. Consequences - consequences!

God as judge is not a concept with which modern western Christians sit comfortably. A kind of hidden universalism permeates many churches. Many still would give lip service to there being a hell but there is little about how they live and the urgency they have in telling others that suggests they really believe it. Some honestly admit to universalism and desperately try to find an acceptable hermeneutic to make it biblically OK. Thus scripture is twisted and reinterpreted to the point where it is proposed as saying the opposite of what it does say to make everything alright. Others who know you can't twist scripture this way just keep quiet about such things preferring to avoid the issue so they can believe what they would like to believe without being challenged.

So it is that large parts of the church no longer believe in the reality of hell. Thus the church loses its prophetic edge and a whole society loses any fear of judgement. This in turn impacts moral choices, many throwing themselves into ever deeper hedonism on the basis that either sin isn't real or if it is God will see us alright in the end.

It is important to understand that God as Trinity has a direct bearing on how we should conduct relationships within the Kingdom and therefore on how we do church. Please understand that we are not suggesting, as some do, that leadership and authority have no part to play in church life. They manifestly do but that authority is about calling and function not status, and that leadership must centre in servanthood not control. Jesus, whilst on earth, humbled Himself under the authority of the Father, which did not make Him in any way lesser.

Paul's teaching about mutually submitting to one another is modelled on the basis of how God functions. We ignore this and reap the consequences. Despotic church leaders begin to rule, insisting on obedience and manipulating weak Christians to their own (often well intentioned) ends. When the church moves that way, once again its prophetic edge is blunted and national secular structures become more despotic. We can see this pattern clearly in many western government structures.

A poor understanding of God brings about a tendency to set ourselves up as His judge. We look at how He has operated over the centuries and weigh what He has done against the popular ‘morality’ of the day. He doesn’t step in and stop all suffering so many decide He must be limited or flawed. His teaching, revealed consistently in Old and New Testaments, doesn’t fit with what we decide is right, for example in the realm of homosexual relationships or the pursuit of happiness, so we decide that He is wrong or has been misrepresented. A faulty understanding of God inevitably leads to human beings setting themselves up as the ultimate purpose of existence and from that fundamental error all chaos breaks out.

Our belief about God has consequences, good or bad and if we are adequately to deal with the bad consequences we need to adjust the foundational understanding. A dying world desperately needs it.

Chapter 2

The Truth About Humanity

Myrtle meant well. She longed to be loved. Her father had disappeared when she was ten years old and her mother had clung to her, an only child, in her emotional need. Sadly the clinging lasted too long. As years went by Myrtle realised, though couldn't find the words to explain it, that her mother was using her for her own self-centred needs. It ended in a huge row and she stormed out, making the occasional phone call but never going to see her Mum again except for one Christmas when her mother's reaction was a combination of stifling affection and blame for all her own problems.

She was nineteen when she left home and twenty-six when she first went to a church in the hope that she might find something real there. She lapped up the idea of grace and God forgiving her and quickly was baptised. Almost as quickly she won the heart of Martin. After five years and two children the fault lines in the relationship became obvious. Every time Martin went away on business she was edgy. She expected many phone calls each day and imagined all sorts of things if they were not as frequent as she wanted. She hated having to spend time with his parents and with his sister's family. She made none too subtle attempts to stop it happening.

Excess money was spent on the children but noticeably more on the daughter than the son. The daughter, Millie, loved all the attention and knew how to demand more. Myrtle lived in terror of being abandoned by husband and daughter and thought little of their son, Maurice.

How the situations above ended is not the point for our purposes but it is an ongoing journey. Some would see in this tale as evidence that we are not responsible for many of our actions but are helpless victims of how others have treated us. Indeed much modern psychology would encourage this 'I am a victim' mentality. There is a more foundational point to be made, however, and that is that all people are not what they should be and often mistake the urgency of the meeting of their own emotional needs for the building blocks of love.

This disconnect between what we are and what we should be is present in all human beings and manifests itself most obviously in the areas in which we are most damaged.

Perhaps there is no clearer evidence of the serious link between, truth, its application and the consequences we make in the light of it than when we consider the truth about human beings. Our starting point of understanding with regard to humanity will have a huge impact upon how we regard ourselves and other people and this in turn is an issue at the root of many of the key moral issues and behavioural problems, not just of our age but every age.

Truth.

The bible is clear. Human beings, both men and women, are the creation of God. Not only are we created by God but also we are, uniquely, created in His image. Humanity is the high watermark of creation. Humanity was created to rule over those aspects of creation that are to be found on this earth. Adam was given the job of naming other creatures and was to rule over them. The commission was to ***'fill the earth and subdue it'***. The task of our first parents was to take what they enjoyed in Eden and make the rest of the world just like it. The earth, its animals and its fruit were to be at the disposal of mankind and, in turn, humans were to care for this creation and develop it as stewards in the service of God.

Another truth from the bible is that humanity was created male and female. Eve was created from Adam making it clear that they were not separate from one another but a part of one another. The word, rather weakly translated 'helper' in the NIV (Gen 2:20) in reality has a much more profound meaning. It is a word formed from two Hebrew words, one meaning 'called to bring strength' and the other 'face to face'. Man and woman together are portrayed as a glorious partnership, needing one another to be complete. They were made to enjoy God's presence; to walk in an unhindered and unobscured closeness of relationship with Him, enjoying His provision and fulfilling His calling.

Though made in the image of God human beings, both men and women, are sinful. They were not created that way but became that way by choosing to do the one thing that God had forbidden them to do. This act of rebellion seriously damaged that image of God in which we were made and all humanity from then on has been tainted with a sinful nature and a propensity to rebel. The consequences of this first act of sin are wide ranging. There was ejection from the garden so that they could not eat from the fruit of the tree of life, awareness of good and evil without the capacity to handle that awareness, shame at nakedness, pain in childbirth, the rule of male over female, sweaty toil in producing food and physical decline and death, the body returning to the dust from which it was made.

Much more could be said but what we have identified so far is enough to move on to how these truths should be applied to everyday life and the consequences that will come from our choices regarding that application.

Application.

If human beings are the creation of God then it follows that He has rights over us. Yet we live in a world where we regularly hear the statement, 'no-one has any right to tell me what to do.' We are not masters of the universe and not even masters of our own lives and destiny. Our purpose in existing must spring from God's desires rather than our own. Also it becomes clear that we have greater value than the rest of this earth's creations. We alone bear God's image and have been given authority over animal life, plant life and even the earth itself to exercise in line with God's purposes. We are not servants of 'mother earth' but authoritative stewards placed here by God to care for His creation. The fact of sin entering the equation does not take away our calling. So it is that Jesus applies the same truth in terms of the Kingdom of God through the great commission **(Matthew 28:16-20)** with the calling to go into all the world and make disciples.

It is clear that the biblical view sees man and woman together. Adam was created first but there is no hint in the creation story of that giving him superiority. Rather in face to face partnership they are to fulfil God's calling. The coming together of a man and woman in marriage gives testimony to the origin of being one flesh, intrinsically belonging together. The physical coming together in sexual union is a picture of completeness as man and woman are designed to fit together face to face. This is not to pretend that man and woman are identical in how they fulfil their part in their joint calling but each of the two parts is for the same end and in the closest of imaginable partnerships. Paul likens this union to that between Christ and His church **(Ephesians 5:30-33)**. One product of the entry of sin (the Fall) is that this male female relationship has been dislocated to some extent. This has resulted in the concept of the man ruling over the woman and, we believe, the reactionary product of the concept of female supremacy.

All this has a knock on effect to how we conduct ourselves in the church context. Whatever our theological position regarding the appropriateness or otherwise of women in an eldership role, it is clear that we cannot claim they are barred because a man should rule over a woman. Yes we are products of the fall but the church is the redeemed community of God and salvation in Jesus Christ restores what was lost at the fall. There is a healthy debate to be had about male and female roles in church life but it cannot be allowed to be about rule (imposed authority) for that would be a denial of the Gospel.

Another product of the fall is that in some cases ***'Even their women exchanged natural relations for unnatural ones. In the same way the men also abandoned natural relations with women and were inflamed with lust for one another. Men conducted indecent acts with other men, and received in themselves the penalty of their perversion'*** (Romans 1:26-27).

At the time of writing this the government of Great Britain has recently passed a law allowing same sex marriage. The secular voice and homosexual lobby has shouted loudest and appears to be winning the day. For now we must simply point out that the bible (consistently) declares sexually active homosexual relationships to be sinful and the bible is not going to go away, despite astonishingly convoluted attempts to claim it says the opposite of what it does.

Instinctively we all know that things aren't as they were meant to be. No matter how much we encounter death, even in old age, it does not feel fully natural. Many are burdened with a sense of shame and they can't quite work out where is comes from. People feel guilty and although sometimes it is obvious why this is, at other times the feeling is just there. This is because we are guilty and can't understand what to do with that guilt.

Consequences

We all have to make choices in the light of truth. We can accept what scripture teaches or reject it. We can accept it in theory but in practice become selective about which bits we will respond to or turn a blind eye to some parts of scripture and pretend they are not there. Every choice we make brings with it consequences.

If we are made by God then His owner's rights need to be more than notional. We are faced with a task of finding out what He requires of us to try to put it into practice. This is serious stuff. He is the one who told us to have no other gods except Him. He told us not to make a graven image, not to steal, murder or commit adultery. He tells us to love Him with all our heart mind, soul and strength and to love our neighbour as ourselves. We are made for Him and in His image. This brings a responsibility to work at making this world a better place. In the context of New Testament Kingdom teaching we are to bring His Kingdom to bear on the Kingdom of darkness. Thus living for self-interest and pleasure cannot be an option. Pastorally we have found that the very people who are most desperate to know fulfilment are the ones who live to satisfy their own perceived needs and the ones who are least preoccupied with these perceived needs are the most fulfilled.

Myrtle desperately needed to be grounded in biblical truth about her own humanity. She needed to know that love has its model in God. She needed to know that she, her husband, her children and her parents were all damaged goods that needed healing. The only hope of healing was to get her head (and heart) around a biblical view of what human beings are and how to seek to love selflessly.

If we choose to see each person as the creation of God, made in His image, we will place on them great value and indeed recognise our own value. If we choose to see humanity as the accidental outcome of chaotic chemical collisions then, although some may choose to give human life value, there is no intrinsic reason to do so. Thus people become expendable to satisfy our whims, whether it is the pole dancer who is ogled, the prostitute who is used, the child who is bullied, the woman (man) brought into the lust ridden bed until they become wearying, the people of another race that we choose to see as less than fully human or whatever.

Whenever human beings are used to satisfy others, it is at root because they are not valued and are objectified. Having made clear our belief that homosexual activity is sinful we also need to make clear that this in no sense justifies anyone in treating those involved in that activity without respect, compassion and grace, whilst not compromising with truth. This is equally true of those who choose a lifestyle of heterosexual promiscuity or other wrong practices. All sinners (therefore all of us) are made in God's image and their intrinsic value stems from this.

Over the years there have been tragic consequences that have sprung from failing to recognise what it is that gives human beings unique worth. A view of humanity that fails to recognise God's initiative is hard pressed to give any coherent reason to value that humanity. So it was that in Nazi Germany the disabled and the less than racially 'pure' were regarded as expendable. In our own culture the same underlying philosophy lies at the heart of our casual attitude to abortion and the growing demand for mercy killing and euthanasia. Equally truly, though less obviously, that attitude also lies at the heart of our society's manic drive to get people out to work and expect them to work ever harder as wealth creation becomes more important than human wellbeing.

We create a society in which women are given financial inducement to have their young children 'minded' while they go out to work and penalise those mothers who wish to care for their own children, then we the scratch our heads wondering why behavioural standards and mental health issues in the young are so concerning.

If we make the choice to deny or downplay the reality of human sinful nature we reap the consequences of failing to find answers that satisfy the human dilemma. If a house across the road bursts into flames and you heroically run towards it to rescue the person appearing at an upstairs window, you do a good thing. If on the way you begin to think that by doing so you might become famous with your name in the papers, the action becomes tarnished. It is still good but that is not the whole story. All people find even their best moments marred with the less than good. Failure to see that this is a root problem leads to successive governments and educational systems making policy on the assumption that human nature is good.

Surely there are enough horrors across the world, down our street and even in our own actions to make this idea ridiculous. Sin needs addressing and Jesus came to address it. Forgiveness, discipline and divine power to gain victory over the sinful nature are needed. When we fail to recognise this we fail even to attempt to deal with the root of the human problem.

We have choices to make about how men and women co-exist in this world. To see them as two aspects of the one whole leads to very different practices than seeing them as intrinsically separate. In Christ there is neither Jew nor Gentile, slave nor free, male nor female.

We see right at the beginning in the Garden of Eden how sin brought separation; separation between God and Man, between Adam and Eve and that has continued. Therefore to a large extent we live in an individualistic world that feeds our independence and separation. We hear and use the terms 'human rights' or 'my rights' in all areas of life. This thinking polarises rather than unites. So we have battles between nations, employees and employers, men and women.

Jesus came to bring down barriers but to do that He had to deal with the root problem, which is sin in the human heart. Through His death on the cross He paid the price of our sin before God and through His resurrection broke the power of sin that had been holding this world captive. Through Christ we enter the Kingdom of God where brokenness and division play no part. Jesus fills us with the Holy Spirit and leads us into a unity of heart and mind where we can love one another.

The temptation to think that in following Christ we have to right every wrong in the world and solve every problem is huge. What we need to understand is that the only answer to this world's ills is Jesus and our prime calling is to love the world, make Him known and demonstrate His coming Kingdom.

We will still belong to different nations with different histories, cultures and customs but now because we are in Christ we can love and accept, even embrace our differences rather than be upset by them. We will still have those in authority and those under authority (slave or free) but rather than be at war we can love appreciate and care for one another in God's Kingdom where we all live under His Lordship. We still have male and female but now we are able to bring the uniqueness of our manhood and womanhood (equal but complementary) into God's Kingdom.

This manifestly does not mean that men and women no longer exist as separate entities. Otherwise teaching on marriage and Pauls' teaching on how women and men at different stages of their lives should be treated would be pointless. Also whatever the more debated verses about men women and authority are all about they do indicate that the male-female difference is recognised in more than biological terms. However, it certainly means that all are the same in terms of salvation and even 'sonship' in that both equally inherit all things in Christ. Biblically the centrality of male and female belonging together needs to find expression in how we live our lives. There are choices to be made and these choices will have differing consequences even among those who agree on the underlying theology. Some will be male only elder/minister led. Some will be male and female elder/minister led and some will be married couple only elder/minister led. The debate will go on but it is essential we root our choices in our understanding of biblical truth.

There is always pressure on the church to bend to conform to prevailing attitudes in the culture in which it is placed. This can be fine when it comes to things like time keeping. Many of us in England have had to adjust to the increasing phenomenon of worshippers arriving (and leaving) at various points in our meetings. It is not fine in other areas. A culture may be polygamous but the church, although having to work with the reality, must be a prophetic voice into that culture declaring a better way. A culture may have a tendency to major on disciplining children by beating them. Physical discipline in our view does have a place but the beating of a child is not right and would not be right even if every person in that region believed it was. So in our British life today society may have bought into the acceptance of promiscuity and may want to celebrate homosexual activity. If the church accepts that, it places itself at variance with scripture and under God's judgment. If it chooses a different way and opts to be a prophetic voice for change then it will be ridiculed and probably persecuted. We know which we would rather face!

Our underlying beliefs always have profound consequences. There are dangers that come from having a faulty understanding of humanity but there are also clear dangers in not having thought through the issues at all, for then we become those who are blown this way and that by the popular view of the day or intimidated by those who shout the loudest and bully the most. It is time for Christians to think with their bibles open and begin to recognise that how we perceive truth brings massive consequences.

Chapter 3

The Truth About The Cross

'Oh' said Mary, 'I love to read about Jesus but I hate the bit about all that suffering and blood.'

Kirk liked to ask everyone, 'are you washed in the blood?' He found it odd that even Christians didn't like to answer him.

At the heart of the Christian Gospel is the cross of Jesus Christ. Many have commented on the oddity of an instrument of common execution becoming the most well-known symbol of the Christian faith. Although many have tried to develop a concept of Christian faith that marginalises the cross they have never succeeded because even a casual reading of the New Testament brings us back to its importance. In each of the four Gospels a huge amount of space is given to the last week of Jesus' life and in particular His death and subsequent resurrection. Also Paul's letters return again and again to the centrality of the cross. Paul wrote to the Corinthians: ***'For I resolved to know nothing while I was with you except Jesus and Him crucified.'*** (1 Corinthians 2:2). Here Paul actually contrasts the 'foolishness' and simplicity of his message with clever philosophy. However uncomfortable some may find it, a form of Christianity which sidelines the cross is not really Christianity at all.

Truth

The obvious truth of scripture is that the death of Jesus on the cross is central to the message that we are called to believe and proclaim. It is also clear that somehow the salvation of human beings from the damage done by sin and opportunity of eternal life is only possible because of the cross. So far few who hold to Christian faith would disagree. However, it is how the cross brings about this salvation that causes many who claim the name of Jesus Christ to be at odds with each other and in some cases quite vehemently. To deal with these issues thoroughly would take a book in itself but we wish to make some points that seem clear to us.

There is little disagreement that the cross is the supreme demonstration of God's love **(Romans 5:8)**. It is also fairly well agreed that this sacrifice of love is a great example of being selfless that we should all seek to live up to. However, when we get to the idea of a redemption price being paid, Jesus dying in our place for our sin (substitutionary atonement) and the wrath of God being appeased many find themselves somewhat revolted and cannot accept some or all of these concepts. Thus we have some Christian leaders now calling the doctrine of substitutionary atonement the equivalent of cosmic child abuse!

The problem is that all these concepts and more can be found in New Testament teaching and to suggest that they, or some of them, are culturally limited to the time and we, as the more enlightened, have moved on from such concepts will not do. We would suddenly find ourselves amongst those who were criticising Paul for his simple and crude message of the cross preferring to ours on their own superior wisdom.

The models of atonement through the cross that we find in the New Testament are not given as preferred options from which we are to choose but as necessary understandings that together give us as full a grasp as possible of what the cross was all about. The Passover lamb, the redemption price being paid, the judge declaring us 'not guilty' and being freed from slavery are all important images of a truth no one of them can fully contain. **See John 1:29, 1 Corinthians 5:7, Acts 20:28, Romans 3:24, John 8:36, Galatians 5:1.**

The concept that God was in Christ reconciling the world to Himself (a concept that makes a nonsense of the cosmic child abuse charge) reveals that each of these pictures the New Testament paints of atonement through the cross are inadequate without the others. Even when taken all together we should have the humility to accept that our understanding will not be complete.

Application

We are faced with the need to be biblical in our understanding. The fact that one of the New Testament pictures of atonement through the cross may appeal to us more is no excuse for using it to the exclusion of others. To bypass the centrality of the cross and suggest it is merely a great example of selfless love and nothing more rips the heart out of the Christian message and leaves sin not dealt with. If Jesus did not need to die for our salvation it makes His death a cruel sideline perpetrated either by a sadistic God or by human beings with God not being active in it at all. The only justification for what happened to Jesus is that His death was absolutely necessary for a loving God to rescue human beings.

If we seek to be a people who are committed to the scriptures as our supreme authority for belief and practice then we are not at liberty to minimise the significance of any one aspect of atonement teaching. That we find some of it confusing does not mean that we should leave it untaught. That we find some of it offensive, such as the wrath of God being appeased, ought not to surprise us as there are enough warnings in scripture that the cross is offensive to the natural mind.

However, this principle applies equally to those who seem to think that the appeasement of God and substitutionary atonement are the only 'legitimate' ways of viewing the cross. Certainly without them the picture is incomplete but that is also true of every aspect of teaching about the cross in the New Testament. Sometimes our feeling that we need to have a systematic theology that makes it all fit together does not let the scripture speak freely and imprisons it in our own self comforting orthodoxy.

Consequences

The consequences of getting this wrong are potentially very grave. On the one hand we can run the risk of people accepting, in repentance and faith, the salvation brought through the cross, knowing that their sin is atoned for but never fully grasping that God loves them intimately. His love is reduced to a blanket concept which took Jesus to the cross. They lose sight of 1 John 3:1: ***'How great is the love the Father has lavished on us, that we should be called children of God!'***

On the other hand people are introduced to a God who loves them too much to do them any harm, the cross being just an example of God loving. The dreadfulness of sin is minimised, the prospect of hell ignored and the underlying problem of our guilt never addressed. The end result is a tortured life of feeling guilty because we are and yet our theological base telling us we are not. The capacity for someone to be made clean by the blood of Jesus is regarded as antiquated and repulsive so they are never made clean because that is the only way.

Another consequence regarding the choices we make in this area centres in what happens to how we view the bible. If, on so central an issue as this, it is OK to pick and choose then surely it must be on every issue. As we have pointed out earlier, once we begin to depart from scripture as our basic template for living chaos ensues and the generation that comes after us are at best short changed and at worst led down a blind alley.

Chapter 4

The Truth About Church

Don took his church very seriously. He sometimes missed a Sunday meeting but was never missing when there was discussion about the business of the church. He did his bit by acting as a steward sometimes and if a choir was formed he liked to sing. He had been a leader in the church but had resigned because the other leaders could not see what was best for the church. The new full time pastor (he had been there two years) was beginning to do dangerous things in his eyes. Don didn't like the new style home groups where people were encouraged to open up to each other. He didn't like the more informal worship and above all he didn't like the fact that some folk were being given responsibilities without the explicit agreement of the church members.

He couldn't see that his discomfort stemmed from the fact that things were happening that he could not control. He wrote the pastor a letter advising him to change his ways or he would see that his ministry was a short one. It even included the phrase, 'if you don't think I can do this ask your predecessor why he left'.

Sally was part of the wider leadership of the church. She thought the new pastor was wonderful and supported him to the full. In return she expected him to appoint her to the new proposed role of pastor's personal secretary. She could think of nothing better than to be with him so much. Of course it would stay deeply spiritual. She was angry when he did not ask her to consider the role and told him so very clearly.

Morgan was the new pastor. He did not believe himself to be infallible and had tried hard to get everyone 'onside' as he attempted to take the church in what he believed was the right direction. Don and Sally were only two people amongst a greater number who all wanted things to work their way. There were others who loved to gossip. Morgan was a resilient character but he was beginning to feel the pressure and he began to be nervous of Sundays and be close to breaking point when there were meetings to discuss church business. His wife, Molly, still made it on a Sunday but refused to come to any other meetings. She spent many an hour in tears. She felt guilty for adding to Morgan's problems and he felt guilty for allowing a situation that had brought her to such a stressful condition.

Church is a word often used and seldom understood. It is a subject few think about with any seriousness and those that do are often regarded as 'sad cases'. Yet the church, according to the bible, is one of the few realities in this life which continues into the next. It is also impossible to understand God's purposes to any significant level without considering the church.

Truth.

The Greek word *ecclesia*, from which we get our word 'church', has the basic meaning of a group of people set apart for a specific purpose. Thus the church of Jesus Christ is a group set apart for Him. What the bible has to say about church is mainly found in the writings of Paul, Peter and John. Jesus had little to say about it directly but that ought not to surprise us, as it did not begin until after His death and resurrection.

In **Romans 9-11** Paul carefully explains how the church has taken over from Israel as the inheritor of the promises of God, the true Israel being those of the New Covenant which is by faith rather than the Old Covenant of law. Although we do not believe, as some do, that God has therefore no future for His ancient people it is clear that the end time promises of God to His ancient people now apply to the church either exclusively or as well. Jesus does speak of the church in **Matthew 16:18**, telling His disciples that He will build His church and the gates of hell will not overcome it. He is the rock on which the church is to be built. He also mentions it in passing when speaking of what to do with a brother who has sinned against you. However, it is also fair to apply **John 20:20-26** to the church as He prays that we might be brought to complete unity and see His glory.

The three key images of the church that unfold through the writings of Peter and Paul are those of body, temple and bride.

In **1 Corinthians 12-14** Paul describes the church as the body of Christ with each member a key part; like parts of a human body. Christ is the head and each part is to do its work, empowered by the Holy Spirit, using the spiritual gifts that God provides and dominated by loving commitment.

In **1 Corinthians 3:16** Paul describes this body as a temple of God. That is where God lives by His Spirit. In **1 Corinthians 6:19** he breaks it down to each of our own physical bodies also being a temple of the Holy Spirit and so they should not be used for unholy purposes. Peter develops this idea of church as the temple of God in **1 Peter 2:4-10**. He describes the church both as a spiritual house but also as the Holy Priesthood in that house which makes spiritual sacrifices. In quick succession he identifies the church as a spiritual house, a chosen people, a royal priesthood, a holy nation and a people belonging to God – all these to declare His praises. He is clearly drawing on imagery from Old Testament temple worship.

The third key image is that of bride. The church is the bride of Christ. In **Ephesians 5:31-32** Paul speaks of a man and a woman becoming one flesh and then applies it to Christ and the church calling it a profound mystery. In the parable of the ten bridesmaids Jesus seems to put Himself in the position of the groom. Gloriously **Revelation 21** describes the church as the New Jerusalem coming down out of heaven as the spotless bride prepared for the Lamb of God. This image speaks of deepest intimacy of relationship and love. It speaks of destiny and fulfilment.

Much more could be written about the church but we have enough for our purposes and can now turn our minds to application.

Application.

The first thing to stress is how central the church is to God's plan, to His Kingdom (of which the church is to be a model and vanguard) and to individual salvation. The bible knows nothing of an individualistic salvation that ignores the church. Individuals are saved into the community of faith and are expected to express their discipleship in the context of that community. The values of the Kingdom, of grace, mercy, holiness, forgiveness and love are to be modelled by the church. The church is meant to be a prophetic demonstration of the Kingdom of God and be central and vital to all our lives! The church is God's tool in the power of the Spirit for the bringing in of His Kingdom to an ever increasing measure. The local, regional and worldwide expressions of the church (all biblical concepts) share this task. The church of Jesus Christ is the only hope for the world. There is no plan B!

As we look at the biblical images of the church we can see that the church is to be a mutually dependent concern, each part having a role to play but needing all the other parts. No part has cause to consider itself more important than another. There is no place for envy, hunger for power or selfish individualism. The Kingdom and the church are to be the new first loyalty, superseding all others. Our ethnic origin and nationality take second place to our new identity as citizens of the Kingdom of God. Even our natural earthly families are to take a secondary place (a hard truth to swallow). **See Luke 14:26 & Matthew 12:47-50**. We are called to model the fact that in Jesus every earthly barrier that separates us is destroyed!

The hallmark of the Saviour is to be ours – that of service.

As the body of Christ we are called to use the spiritual gifts that God provides and although those outlined in **1 Corinthians 12** are not meant to be exclusive they are meant to be part of normal church experience. Seeking to do God's work as the body of Christ but ignoring the gifts He gives for the task (the tools for the job) is folly. These gifts have a primary application to the church moving out, being used in the cut and thrust of everyday life and mission.

The image of the temple reminds us that we are an indwelt people. The Spirit of God lives within.

We are set apart for Him and are therefore set apart for holiness. When parts of the church enter into sinful activities, the whole church is tarnished and God's name is cheapened. Holiness of life is our calling and that means a radical commitment to putting into practice the apostles' teaching as we find it in the New Testament.

As the bride we are to be besotted with Jesus looking eagerly for His return when He will finally claim us as His own. We are not to live mechanistically but in deep intimacy of love with our Saviour through the Holy Spirit.

Consequences

Looking at the above it is fair to say that the church frequently falls a long way short of its calling. This is due to the consequences of wrong choices. Sacramentalists have often reduced our salvation to a mechanism through ritual. Evangelicals have often reduced it to making a decision to follow Christ and getting individually saved. Sacraments, decision making and personal salvation all are of major importance but even together they are not the whole picture. By choosing to limit what salvation is we have bypassed the church making it an unappealing intrusion into our lives. Our destiny is together and until we properly express our faith together we will always fail to see the glory of the church. Our choices bring consequences.

Within the body we are called to live in mutual accountability. We choose not to and damage ourselves spiritually as well as hinder the church. When we choose to ignore the spiritual gifts we disempower the church and ourselves. A church that seeks to fulfil God's humanly impossible calling using natural talents and human resources alone is bound to become frustrated and largely impotent. Use the tools well and we will be effective. Fail to use them and we will be ineffective. Similarly seeing spiritual gifts for use mainly as we worship together will create a self-indulgent church with all the dangers of spiritual incest.

To hive off into our monocultural, single nationality sub groups will not do. If we model how every barrier comes down in Jesus we are a prophetic voice to the world. If we do not, we reinforce separation and suspicion. To choose our natural families as a priority over God's people not only suggests we see this 'one body' idea as only notional, it also sends a clear signal to the next generation that church is a side issue. It must be said that all this does not justify our neglect of our natural families. They are a sacred trust from God but need to find their place in His wider purposes.

As the temple we are called to live in holiness. We choose to see this as unattainable because we want to keep a toehold or more in sinful pleasures. As a result our message lacks authenticity, our consciences are troubled and our power very limited.

As the bride we are called to intimacy but all too often reduce worship to formality, devotional activity to duty and prayer to a shopping list. In the process we short-change the next generation by pretending there is no more of God to be experienced. Choices!

We are called to love Him with every fibre of our being and He is found by those who seek Him with all their heart.

Don, Sally, Morgan and Molly all need to know what church is meant to be. We desperately need people to be taught the truth and shown how to apply it. We need to help them to make the choices of building up, encouragement and love. The consequences of wrong choices are not hard to see. The consequences of right choices will be very different.

We have to make choices about how church functions and for the most part we tend to adopt human, mechanistic ways of organising church because they are easier to manage. We have yet to encounter a church that takes seriously the five-fold ministries of **Ephesians 4**. Principles are sometimes derived from this passage but seldom is it fully used as it is clearly meant to be – a biblical pattern of church structure. Paul is clear that to choose it leads to stability, security and wisdom. To refuse it leads to being blown around by every wind of doctrine; a description that seems to fit our day very well.

Looking at the Church in Britain today it seems obvious that we are reaping the consequences of poor choices. Repentance and change is needed.

Chapter 5
The Truth About The Kingdom

'We shouldn't talk so much about the Kingdom because it conveys the idea of warfare and crusades. It's just not appropriate these days.' So said Carolyn.

Stan, on the other hand, would say, 'I look forward to the day when I can enter God's Kingdom for then the pain of this life will be over and I will be in glory.'

However, Paula would be likely to say, 'I am so glad we have come to understand that God's kingdom is here. We have wasted so much time talking about heaven to come and it's just not helpful.

Whereas Harry was clear in His understanding. 'Yes I know the bible mentions the Kingdom but the Gospel is really about personal salvation and getting people to heaven.'

The Kingdom of God is an often misunderstood subject with people having a whole variety of ideas as to what it means; many of them rooted in tradition and a lack of biblical understanding. Everywhere Jesus went He proclaimed the Gospel (Good News) of the Kingdom. In **Matthew 24:14** Jesus says, ***And this gospel of the kingdom will be preached in the whole world as a testimony to all nations, and then the end will come.*** We would do well then to know what the bible means when it talks of the Kingdom of God and see how it affects us and if we have any part to play in its outworking.

Truth.

In the New Testament the term Kingdom of God and Kingdom of Heaven are used interchangeably. The Jews didn't like to use the Name of God and so often used the term Kingdom of Heaven instead. Simply put the Kingdom of Heaven/God is wherever the Rule of God is displayed and enjoyed. In **Matthew 6:9-10** when the disciples asked Jesus to teach them to pray He started His teaching by having as of first importance a focus on the Holiness of God the Father and that His Kingdom should come and His will be done on earth as it is in heaven.

It is clear then that God's Kingdom is in Heaven and there He rules and reigns completely, His will being done all the time. And it is also clear that God's desire is that His rule, reign and will be done on earth too.

In **Mark 1:9-14** we read about the Baptism of Jesus and how immediately after His Baptism the Holy Spirit, who had descended on Him in the form of a dove and remained on Him lead Jesus out into the wilderness where He was tempted of the devil for 40 days. When Jesus came back from the wilderness to Galilee He immediately began preaching the good news, saying that the moment had come for which all of history had been waiting. God's Kingdom had come to the earth. Kingdom invasion had begun!

The Garden of Eden had been this amazing place of existence where everything was perfect, where God ruled supreme and Adam and Eve lived in perfect relationship with him. In that environment there was no death, sickness, pain or sorrow. But then because of their sin mankind was cast out of the garden, cast out from the place of God's presence. Mankind was excluded from God's

Kingdom rule and so death, sickness, pain and sorrow came into the world.

But as we read through the scriptures it becomes very evident that God still desired to be with mankind, to dwell with them. But for that to happen our sin, our self-centeredness, our self-reliance, and our independence from God had to be dealt with. And so God chooses a people for Himself, starting with a man called Abram.

In the early chapters of the Old Testament we follow the growth and development of this people who belonged to God. God wanted to be with His people and once they escaped from slavery in Egypt He began to be with them in a special way. He had Moses make a tent called a tabernacle where He could dwell. And so His presence and Kingdom is seen again in the Holy of Holies, in the tabernacle among His people. For the children of Israel this continued for 40 years as they wandered from place to place and then they entered the Promised Land and eventually they built the temple in Jerusalem. The design of the temple was the same as the tabernacle, the outer court, the inner court and the Holy of Holies. God's presence was among His people but still only in a small room, only the high priest could enter that place and then only once a year. In that place God dwelt, in that place was His

Kingdom rule but what good was that small room for the whole world?

Even the People of God couldn't enjoy the Kingdom as they were excluded from the room where God lived and only in the other rooms could animal sacrifices take place to deal with their sin. They continued to walk in disobedience to God and eventually God allowed them to be taken into captivity, the temple was destroyed and even the little room was gone! What hope now?

But God was working out His plans, after 70 years the people of God were allowed back to Jerusalem and eventually the temple was rebuilt and it is at that time in history Jesus, the Son of God is born in Bethlehem.

The fulfilment of the ages is fast approaching. God's perfect plan for this world is being worked out. And then in **Mark 1:15** we read how Jesus comes back to Galilee from the 40 days of temptation in the wilderness and He is saying, 'The time has come'. 'The Kingdom of God is at hand, right here, right now!!

This is it, this is what the world has been waiting for!'

Where was the Kingdom and presence of God now? Right there wherever Jesus was. God was now walking the earth as a man full of the Holy Spirit. And so Jesus is saying 'repent, turn away from your old life. Turn to me and I will give you

Life with a capital L'. Luke 4:14 tells us that Jesus returned in the power of the Spirit to Galilee, and a report about him went out through all the surrounding country.

People were talking about Jesus. He was the talk of the whole area! It seems that everywhere He went He demonstrated the presence of God and the Kingdom of God by healing the sick, working miracles, casting out demons and even raising the dead. History would never be the same again. God's Kingdom had broken into this world in a new way. And when we get to Pentecost after Jesus death, resurrection and ascension back to heaven Jesus pours out the Holy Spirit of God upon all those who had put their trust in Him.

Now, He, the Holy Spirit of God who had come and rested on Jesus in the form of a dove came upon the people of God gathered in an upper room. This time though He didn't come as a dove but came with tongues of cleansing fire. Now the presence of God and the Kingdom of God was poured into the hearts and lives of the people of God who were the Church.

Now we, the Church are carriers of the presence of God. Now we, the Church are to demonstrate the Kingdom of God wherever we go just like Jesus did.

Application.

Applying these truths is not difficult to express but they can be difficult to carry out. At root we are called to trust God in every area of life. That includes relationships, family life and parenting, career, material provision etc. and it can be a real challenge. Learning to live a Kingdom lifestyle is what discipleship is all about!

If we go right back to the beginning of the bible and the Garden of Eden before sin had entered the world we find that God made Adam and Eve to be totally free to walk with Him and enjoy life to the full. He told them to be fruitful and increase in number, to fill the earth and subdue it, to take authority and rule over everything that lived.

Adam and Eve had total freedom to live, enjoy and rule as they lived under the blessing and authority of God. They were free as long as they lived in relationship with God. This wasn't law; this was life to the full. They had a dynamic and vibrant relationship with God. So when God said to Adam, ***"You are free to eat from any tree in the garden; but you must not eat from the tree of the knowledge of good and evil, for when you eat from it you will certainly die."*** God wasn't being restrictive, He was protecting them and releasing Adam and Eve into the life He had created them for. That was a life in relationship with God with Him as the Boss, the Lord.

As people who are born again we are now children of God and He is now our Lord, the Boss! As the people of God we take His Kingdom everywhere we go. Into the workplace, the school, the local shops. Our homes are to be places where God rules and reigns because He reigns in our lives.

Sometimes we hear people who have put their trust in Jesus say 'I don't live under the law any more' I can now do what I like, God loves me anyway." That sort of thinking is understandable but it's not Biblical, that is not what Jesus died for, that is not what we are saved for.

In John14:15-16 Jesus says: ***"If you love me, you will keep my commandments. And I will ask the Father, and he will give you another Helper, to be with you for ever.***

Also in what we call the 'Great Commission' in Matthew 28:18-20 Jesus says to His disciples (and us): "***All authority in heaven and on earth has been given to me.*** [19] ***Go therefore and make disciples of all nations, baptizing them in the name of the Father and of the Son and of the Holy Spirit,*** [20] ***teaching them to observe (obey) all that I***

have commanded you. And behold, I am with you always, to the end of the age."

Obedience to Jesus is where true freedom is found. Obedience to Jesus is where we find fulfilment, meaning and Joy. Obedience to Jesus can bring the Kingdom of God into the areas of life that we are involved in. To be a disciple of Jesus is to follow Him, to have Him at the centre of our lives. And He is the Good Shepherd and will lead us into a life worth living.

Obedience to Jesus teaches us to walk away from our old life and step into a new life of Freedom and Joy.

It is such a joy to know we are loved and saved forever.

It is such a joy to know that Jesus is for us and wants to do us good.

It is such a joy to bow the knee, obey and follow where He leads.

As we live this way we become Kingdom bringers into our world.

Consequences

And so we are faced with choices about how we live. We can choose God's way or our own. To choose God's way is where freedom is found. To walk our own way can shipwreck our lives and make us ineffective as children of God. Many a ministry has come to grief as the person concerned has lost sight of the fact that life is about Jesus and His kingdom rather than the search for self-fulfilment. Seeking His Kingdom first is still the only way to move forwards. To fail is to be lost in self-absorption but the more we get it right the more the other issues that crowd our lives will find their place.

Failure to understand the Kingdom also leads to a practical divide between sacred and secular of which the New Testament knows nothing. Personal faith is tolerated by governments as long as it does not impact how we actually live. Thus the guesthouse owners who refuse accommodation to the gay couple are seen as out of order and bigoted. However, it is not only outside the church that this can be a problem. Many regular churchgoers want a devotional faith that does not impact lifestyle choices. So for some they see no incongruity between worshipping 'with all their heart' and having multiple sexual partners. Others sing their praises to God without any understanding that their faith should impact how they conduct their business dealing such as prompt payment of bills and the like. At a more comical level there have been many offended by behaviour in a church building (a sacred place) that they would embrace themselves in the pub. Kingdom means that God no longer is behind the dividing curtain. All is sacred now!

To be wrapped up in Kingdom now to the exclusion of that which is to come will bring deep disappointment because this world remains an unfair place and without the perspective of eternity we can be tempted to claim things that are not true and fall into deception. This is another rock on which ministries have foundered! Alternatively those who fail to grasp the reality of Kingdom now will live with low expectations, continually failing to step out in faith, 'hanging on in there' until they breathe their last and get to heaven! The joy of the adventure with God will largely be lost on them.

The choices we make will bring consequences. We will reap what we sow, even as children of God.

Chapter 6

The Truth About Money

Jerry and Frances were serious about their financial responsibilities towards God. They tithed their income faithfully and made sure tax could be reclaimed on it. They were every church treasurer's dream. However, having done their duty, they were clear that the rest of the money (and there was a great deal) was theirs. They did not respond to special appeals and disapproved of people in church being given a financial helping hand. They felt that if these people tithed properly they would not have any needs.

George and Sally loved coming to church. They worshipped with great enthusiasm, served in many ways and were natural encouragers. Every week they put £5 in the offering and no matter what teaching they heard in financial responsibility it never occurred to them to give more. For them money was not really part of discipleship.

Deirdre was a pensioner. She had never married and although she had distant cousins she regarded the church as her family. She began each month by asking God what she could give to the church and was constantly looking at ways to economise so she could give more. Her home was spotlessly clean but all the furnishings and decor had not been changed for decades. She had three dresses and only bought a new one when one of them could not be repaired. Her only 'extravagance' was her pet cat.

Roger attended every church business discussion. He was appalled that the Pastor was paid a salary nearly as much as his own and opposed its increase every year. He did not believe it was right that church money should be spent unless there was no possible alternative. His wife, Penny, rarely spoke about anything. He gave her an allowance each month and from that she had to run the home, buy birthday presents and the like. He looked after the rest of the money and felt what he did with it was no one else's business, even Penny's.

Graham and Yolande wanted to be wealthy. They believed it was a sign of spiritual blessing and they also believed that if they gave to God's work He was honour bound to give them back a hundred times over. They hadn't seen this happen yet but were still giving to the Tele evangelist, Marlon Mercury, as much as they could. They were waiting in expectation of the great pay off.

It is an odd thing that pieces of paper with no intrinsic value and bits of mainly base metal have become one of the greatest influences of our time. Money in itself has no value but what it represents many would live, die and even kill for. In these increasingly electronic days money is becoming just a notional concept. A plastic card is used or an 'electronic transfer' takes place and money changes hands. Of course it doesn't really. It is simply that the notional wealth which was in the name of the buyer is now transferred to another. When we talk of the truth about money we are really talking in part about the wealth principle; what the old Authorised Version of the bible calls 'mammon'.

Truth

Luke 16:13 and Matthew 6:24 make it clear that we cannot serve both God and money. The verses in Luke just before and after verse 13 give us a helpful context. Trustworthiness in things financial is a sign of how trustworthy we are with true riches. What is most valued among men is detestable in God's sight! Paul tells Timothy that the love of money is a root of all kinds of evil. However, the bible does not describe money itself as evil and gives some clear guidance for its use. What it should not be is the central issue of our lives or our corporate life. **As Psalm 62:10 tells us, *'though your riches increase, do not set your heart on them'*.**

We are to live God-dependently. Any other dependence is basically a form of idolatry. Experience tells us that when people have money they can easily begin to become dependent on it. In **Matthew 19:16-36** Jesus tells the parable of the rich young man and clearly shocks His disciples with the assertion that it is easier for a camel to go through the eye of a needle than for a rich man to enter the Kingdom of God. The young man had become wealth dependent. We should be grateful that Jesus adds the rider that with God all things are possible.

God's heart is to prosper us. Despite the warnings of the danger of abuse the constant witness of scripture is that God wants to bless and prosper His people. When Jesus changed water into wine it was not just the quality of the provision but the quantity that was astonishing. When He fed the 5000 and the 4000 everyone had sufficient to eat (as much as they wanted) and more was left over than was started with! God wanted to prosper the people of Israel. The blessings of obedience in **Deuteronomy 28:1-14** are massive as are the blessings of repentance in **Deuteronomy 30:1-10**. **Matthew 6:25-34** makes it clear that if we seek first God's Kingdom and His righteousness then all the material things that might otherwise cause us worry will be added to us.

So we are called to work by faith in His riches rather than safeguarding our wealth. Failure to do this means that God's blessing, when handled badly, can become our downfall. We have to counteract this by keeping right priorities in focus and that means honouring God with our wealth. Throughout most of the Old Testament the first fruits and the tithe belonged to God. Making that conscious and regular choice was designed to keep people with the right attitude. **Micah 3:6-12** makes a clear link between the people of God bringing the whole tithe and the abundant provision of God being poured out! In **2 Corinthians 9:6-14** Paul reminds us to be generous, systematic and cheerful in our giving. Those who direct the affairs of the church are to be generously provided for, according to **1 Timothy 5:17-18**. A significant part of this prioritising should involve giving to the poor. God's heart for the poor runs throughout scripture. The edges of fields were not to be harvested so the poor could gather grain. When it was being decided what the Gentile church should have to do, remembering the poor was one of the non-negotiables. See Galatians 2:10.

Application.

Applying these truths is not difficult to express but is difficult to carry out. At root we are called to trust God in every area of life and that includes material provision. When we live a comparatively hand to mouth existence that is not so hard. Once when I (Stuart) started a new school the uniform requirements were to cost £50. Our parents at that stage had never had £50 to their name so we prayed about it and a registered post envelope was delivered by the postman shortly afterwards with £50 inside with a note which read: 'I believe you need this'; the name of the sender was not known to us. Living like this, trusting God, was not always easy but frequently practised out of necessity. It is not so easy to have simple expectant faith when there are a few thousand pounds in the bank! So what are we to do?

Here is where the principle of giving becomes crucial. Giving to God what is His due on a regular basis serves as a reminder to us that all we have comes from God and is His! Giving sacrificially puts us again into a position of a measure of human vulnerability where we have to trust God that He will provide. Giving to the poor honours God but also reminds us that we too are dependent on Him for we only have what we are given. All this needs to be done without falling into a legalistic trap where we begin to think that our ritualistic actions somehow are the guarantee of provision, our trust being put in the ritual rather than in God!

We must not become like the rich young man in the parable. These principles are equally valid for us as individuals, as churches and as nations. Capitalism may be the best economic model this world has found to bring prosperity but unregulated and unbridled it is probably the greatest manifestation of the mammon principle the world has ever known.

Having said all this it is clear that we should expect God to prosper us in all sorts of ways. He is the loving and generous Father who encourages us to ask. He is eager to give good gifts to His children and has no mean streak that would lead Him to give a stone when we ask for bread. The more we have and hoard the less we are apt to trust God and therefore miss out on so many blessings by not asking Him!

Consequences

We are faced with choices about what to do with what we have. We can choose God's way or our own. We can be like the rich fool in **Luke 12:13-21** and store up things for ourselves without being rich towards God.

To choose God's way means consciously thanking Him for every material blessing and recognising that it is undeserved. To choose God's way is to make the first fruits available to Him and demonstrate our priorities by tithing what we receive, in our view before the tax man takes his cut! To choose God's way means keeping all we have available to Him and seeking opportunities to be generous as we cheerfully give from our plenty or from our little **(see Luke 21:1-4)**. When we get these choices wrong we end up either building the equivalent of ever larger barns and worrying ourselves sick as to how we can preserve our wealth, or we go to the other extreme and live in unnecessary poverty through assuming we have too little to give to God and hoping our lottery number might come up! As we get things right we should expect God to prosper and bless us. As we seek first the Kingdom we should expect the practical blessing to be ours as well. It is His nature. However, there are choices that can be made in this regard that can take us down a dangerous road.

God prospers us so that we can bless Him and others, not so that we can become bloated with wealth and then proudly declare how spiritual we must be because we are so rich. To see the new luxury car, the new £5,000 watch and the like as a sign of spirituality is a deception of Satan that has been around a long time. Christian leaders have to battle with temptation as much as anyone and when we begin to justify our extravagance by giving it the veneer of spirituality we are on very dangerous ground. We are not arguing for austerity here, just common sense. The pastor who drives to church in his luxury car, wearing his costly watch and top of the range suit whilst surrounded by church folk who struggle every day to keep food on the table is living in deception. He may think he is trying to give his people something to aspire to, if only they can be as spiritual as he is but in reality he is parading ostentation. This behaviour is often accompanied by an authoritarian leadership of the church. That this wealth is produced by the giving of the much poorer members of the congregation is scandalous. Again we do not argue for austerity and no we cannot draw a clear line between what is acceptable and what is not because the real issues lie in the attitude of the heart.

Anyone who cannot walk humbly with God, close to the people and eager to be a servant ought not to be leading a church!

Choices! These must be made and will bring consequences. The choices regarding how we use our money are some of the very big ones. Few things have as much potential to divide or bring together, bless or damage, bring peace or anxiety as the choices we make in this area.

Chapter 7

The Truth About Sex

Colin was a gifted musician and worship leader. He genuinely brought a great sense of God's presence when he led worship and he was highly regarded in the church. He also had a huge problem with on line pornography. He hated himself for it and sought God's forgiveness and strength yet frequently lost the battle. He had sought help. One Christian adviser had told him to find himself a wife and 'use her to deal with his frustrations'. Another had told him not to get hung up on it. It was common and as sins went not too bad. He had huge desires to be God's man and to walk in holiness but was becoming more and more stressed.

Becky was from a lovely Christian home and came to personal commitment to Jesus in her teens. She was serious about her faith and straight down the line on moral issues. That was until she met a man at work called John. He paid her attention and she fell for him hook line and sinker. He began by saying he would do nothing to hinder her faith. He told her he was happy to wait for sex until they were married but his actions and words did not match up and little by little her resistance eroded and a full sexual relationship began. He told her it was only natural and she tried to believe it but her sense of guilt was massive. John tired of Becky soon after and she was so ashamed it made her easy prey to Terry who saw her crying one day and asked what the problem was. She felt safe confiding in Terry as she knew he went to church. He got her to bed with him within 24 hours and then made her swear not to tell anyone because he was married and was actually a leader at his church. Becky eventually found her way back to church but she struggled to forgive herself and although she had one or two boyfriends the relationships were short lived as it became clear she trusted nobody, especially not herself.

Donna was a normal late teenager who loved to come to church though she was still unsure about becoming a Christian. Her friend at school had invited her to a party. There were 'soft drugs' which she dabbled in and toward the end her friend took her to her room and began to play with her sexually. The next day the friend told Donna that she was obviously gay and ought not to hide it. Donna was confused. She had never thought of herself as gay but had been stimulated the previous evening. She thought she liked boys really but was her friend right? She wanted to talk to someone at church but was frightened that she would be ostracised.

Heidi was a lovely young Christian woman. Since coming to faith she had become a radiant example to others. Even her non-Christian husband admitted the change was for the better. She and her husband had two children who came to church with her. Her husband told her that he wanted to experiment sexually and wanted to try other women. Heidi was devastated but prayed and hoped he would see sense. He then said that he wanted to invite some friends round and made it clear that the agenda was one of wife swapping for the night. Heidi was furious and refused. Her husband told her she was unreasonable. Heidi wanted to know what to do. Should she leave her husband? If she did what would happen to her and the boys? She needed advice!

We live in a time in the Western world when we have become sex-obsessed. Not only is this the case but we also have the arrogance to take this idea and read it back into history suggesting that every age and every culture has been sex-obsessed but some just hid the fact more than others. In reality many other cultures and times seem to have handled the issue much more wisely than our own. Years of experience have taught that certain aspects of sexual behaviour damage individuals and whole nations and so it is best to discourage and legislate against them. A sexual free for all makes everyone vulnerable to the financial exploitation of those who would line their pockets by stirring still further lustful desires.

Although the bible has long warned against sexual activity outside the life-long union of a man and a woman, it is also true that most cultures have come to the same conclusion in the light of experience. Sexual activity outside a life-long commitment brings a complexity and confusion to human relationships that are undesirable. Adultery exchanges a brief pleasure for a lifetime of damage. Sexual activity between those of the same sex has been banned by culture after culture in the light of experience. We live in the culture that is arrogant enough to believe that we alone have a better understanding, and the accrued wisdom of the ages is folly before our more enlightened eyes. The development of the birth control pill encouraged people to believe that sexual activity could be without undesirable consequences. Nothing could be further from the truth as we see in the astonishing growth of sexually transmitted diseases, the objectification of others (usually women) and the growth of sexual abuse of both adults and children.

Truth

From the Christian perspective the issue starts at a very basic and foundational place. Is sexual activity a right for the individual to use for his or her own gratification or is it a gift from a loving God to be used according to His guidelines? There is only one biblical answer to this question. To see sexual activity as a right, a matter of personal freedom and choice, is to place others in the position of objects present to gratify our own desires. We may temper this by insisting that others must be willing participants but it still places the emphasis on 'me and my perceived needs'.

That sexual activity can be pleasurable is clearly true but therefore to assume that personal pleasure is its purpose is a dangerous jump in logic. The Christian is faced with a dilemma. Do we adapt to and largely adopt the prevailing view of the day or do we seek to include sexual activity as part of our discipleship? Again there can be only one answer, however hard that may be. Paul makes the point clearly in **1 Corinthians 6:18-20** that our bodies are not our own but are temples of the Holy Spirit. He also makes it clear that sexual sin is unique in that it is against our own bodies.

So what does the bible teach about sex? If we go to **Genesis 2:18** we find God deciding to make a 'helper' for the man. The AV translates this as 'helpmeet' and the original meaning goes much deeper. The word is formed from two words which mean *'one who brings strength'* and *'face to face'*. As the story unfolds we find that sexual activity is there to bring both procreation and intimacy between a man and a woman. This is fundamentally at variance with the idea that sex is for personal pleasure and gratification. These, thankfully, can be by products but the biblical emphasis is on deep intimacy. **'The two shall become one flesh.'** There is also a strong hint here, made clearer in the rest of the bible that children grow best under the parenthood of such an intimate relationship.

So then, unpopular as it may seem, sexual activity is designed to bring the deepest of intimacy to a life-long union and to produce children. That it is pleasurable is a big bonus! However, pleasure is not its purpose except in that it can cement still further the intimacy that God has purposed. The consistent witness of scripture is that sexual activity in any other context is sinful and damaging to those who are involved in it, to those near to them and to society as a whole.

Application

The most clear cut application is to Christians and to the church. If we are serious about discipleship we will be serious about using sexual activity God's way and that means reserving it for marriage – the life-long union of one man and one woman. Of course where people fall short of this and there is genuine repentance there is grace and forgiveness, but it is important we start in the right place. To claim to be disciples of Jesus, walking with Him, while we are in a sexual relationship with someone to whom we are not married is to fool ourselves and the fact that many have been such fools for a time does not diminish the foolishness and sinfulness. We have great sympathy for young people today who are placed under the utmost pressure by a society which propounds very different values but the goal posts are not going to move and we do young people great damage by suggesting they might.

As churches we need to proclaim truth in the context of grace and forgiveness. However, once we start trying to accommodate the prevailing views of our day in a new 'hermeneutic' we are treading on very dangerous ground and doing no favours to individuals, the church or the society in which we live. We are fully aware that the motives of many who wish to find a new way of understanding are those of pastoral concern. Nevertheless, however hard it may seem, we do not do people any good at all by encouraging them to believe their behaviour is OK when the bible consistently says otherwise.

The application to society as a whole is more complex. At root the application is one of judgment, as is always the case where sin is paraded as righteousness. Yet many are caught up in this sex-crazed culture and would love to find a way out. For all the new so-called freedom, many are tortured in themselves, knowing themselves guilty but unsure what they are guilty of, desperately looking for something that will ease their pain and give some glimmer of hope that there might be a meaning to life that goes beyond personal pleasure and the rights of the individual. The church has a responsibility to proclaim a new way, God's way. However, to do so it needs to be much clearer in modelling that way and declaring it with a consistent voice. Individual Christians have a role to play in consistently eroding the false values around by living out different ones in the workplace and in all their relationships.

Consequences

If we, as Christians and as the church, are prepared to rise to the challenge in obedience then the values of the nation can be turned around. It will be slow, painstaking and costly but it can be done in the power of the Holy Spirit. On the other hand if we go down the road of compromise with the prevailing view we will place ourselves under the judgement of God, find our children swiftly reject the faith we espouse and condemn the church to many years of irrelevance.

Christians who insist on rejecting the biblical view of sex will reap in their own bodies and minds the damaging consequences. Those who choose God's way will walk in greater health both physically and mentally.

The mental health impact on society as a whole is one of the less thought about consequences of commonly made choices. The use of sex for personal gratification brings a damaging spread of consequences. The partner subconsciously feels used and objectified. The one seeking the gratification finds it both addictive and yet strangely superficial. The resulting feeling of emptiness plays havoc with the emotions. The inability to understand why this is so plays havoc with the mind. Sometimes for the Christian caught up in such sin the mental torment is greater because there is a measure of understanding as to why the emotions are in turmoil but there is a sense of being trapped in a way of behaving that has become unwantedly compulsive.

Unless it pulls back from the brink the society in which we live, will descend into greater chaos, disease and lawlessness. The consequences of the choices we make are quite stark and of the utmost importance. These are serious times.

Chapter 8

Conditional Promises

The bible contains many promises made to human beings by God. Some are time and occasion specific but many have a timeless principle application, which is very much for us today. A great number of these promises are conditional. In other words God promises to respond if we do certain things. As we bring this book to a conclusion we want to reflect on some of these promises and draw out the some of the consequences of our response.

1. If my people......

In **2 Chronicles 7:11-22** we have the Lord appearing to Solomon after the dedication of the temple. Although the famous promise of verse 14 has a specific application to that particular set of circumstances, we believe there is something of a timeless principle about God and His nature being revealed here.

Our Part:

This applies to those who are the people of God and are called by His name. This seems to us to fit the church.

- Humble ourselves – a right understanding of who God is and who we are. He is Lord and we dare not parade our own 'worthiness'. The implication is that there should be a certain amount of awe as we approach God.
- Pray – address God. Acknowledge His greatness, holiness and glory and plead with Him for the answers we need.
- Seek His face – not a casual exercise but a desire not just to find our answers but to know Him with intimacy.
- Turn from our wicked ways – repent both in heart and action from all we know that falls short of His glory.

God's Part:

- He will hear – not that He is deaf when we speak to Him otherwise but He will hear with a view to response when we do our part.
- He will forgive our sins – a basic principle of scripture is that it is only the penitent that is forgiven. We now know that forgiveness is offered because of the death of Jesus and the fact that He has dealt with sin's consequences. We need to grasp that when God forgives there are no lurking after effects. The slate is wiped clean. This is God's promise.
- He will heal our land – the straightforward transfer of a promise to Israel to a promise to Britain today is not that simple because Israel, the nation, was the people of God and Britain is not. However the application to the church is valid for we are the people of God and inheritors of the promise.

Implications:

If we humble ourselves, pray, seek God's face and turn from our wicked ways He will hear, forgive and heal His church. You might be thinking we are stating the obvious and you would be right! The trouble is the church has become very poor at applying the obvious!

If we do not humble ourselves, pray, seek His face and turn from our wicked ways He will not hear, forgive and heal His church.

Perhaps in our longing for God to move in revival power we have lost sight of the fact there are responses God is looking for in us. The consequences of grasping this or not are quite stark and poles apart. The apparent lack of self-humbling, prayer, God seeking and repentance in the Church in Britain today suggests we have not grasped the point.

2. If you forgive....

In Matthew 6:14-15 Jesus, after teaching the disciples what we now refer to as The Lord's Prayer, makes the unambiguous statement: 'For if you forgive men when they sin against you, your heavenly Father will also forgive you. But if you do not forgive men their sins, your Father will not forgive your sins.' It is worth noting that these words are addressed to His disciples, not the crowds in general. Its context then seems to be how those who belong to the Lord should live. We know that forgiveness comes through faith in Jesus Christ. The implication here is that living as a forgiven people brings with it certain requirements!

Our Part:

Forgive people when they sin against you. When you are wronged forgive!

God's Part:

He will forgive us. Presumably the forgiveness that is ours in Jesus Christ is not blocked.

Implications:

Here we really are resorting to stating the obvious. If we forgive those who wrong us God will forgive us. If we don't He won't! This is very serious stuff. Harbouring resentment and an unforgiving spirit within the life of a Christian or the church is destructive and death bringing.

We need to point out here that we are fully aware that some people have been severely wronged and some of that has been experienced at the hands of Christians and in the church. Some have been shamefully abused and deeply damaged. There have been deep emotional scars. Forgiveness is not saying that such awful behaviour is OK or not serious. To forgive is a choice of will that sometimes is exercised even though the emotions don't feel like forgiving. To harbour unforgiveness only brings harm to the one who harbours it and God wants us to be free. Also to refuse to forgive implies that only those who deserve forgiveness should be forgiven. If this were true we would have no hope of forgiveness from God for we could never deserve it. By refusing to forgive we are missing the whole point of God's grace. This is serious, no matter how hard it is to apply in our day to day living.

3. If you have mustard seed faith.....

In **Matthew 17:20** Jesus tells His disciples that if they have faith as small as a mustard seed they can tell a mountain to move from one place to another and it will move. It is said in response to a question. They wanted to know why they could not drive out a particular demon from a boy. Jesus was clear in His response. They could not do it because they had so little faith.

Our part:

Have faith; even mustard seed size.

God's part:

He will enable mountains to move from one place to another according to what we ask.

It is worth reminding ourselves that this is not faith expressed in a vacuum but faith in Jesus Christ. This suggests we believe He is able to do what we require and is willing to do it and that we expect it to happen.

Implications:

The ability to overcome obstacles in life is dependent on our faith. We tend to get very defensive on such issues. 'Are you suggesting I haven't got enough faith?' someone might ask. The obvious answer is, 'Of course!' We should admit this freely and then seek to grow in faith, in our understanding of it and in our willingness to exercise it. Jesus told the disciples they had not enough faith and yet then said even a tiny amount is enough. This suggests that whom the faith is in is a key as is whether or not we exercise our 'little'.

Any church that seeks to do only what is humanly possible is not really living in faith at all and does not please God. This principle also applies to individual Christians.

The timid Christian learning how to live out their faith and the loud healer who is prone to claiming more than has clearly taken place both need to learn this lesson, as do we all. Faith cannot be about how we feel, about how loud we shout, about how much we declare something to be true even when it is not and so on. Faith has to be absolute trust in Jesus, His power and His willingness; a trust that finds its expression in our words and actions. Where does this kind of trust come from? From spending time with Him until we know Him so well that we sense His priorities and confidently step out in His name. The next promise picks up this theme.

Have you spoken to any mountains recently?

4. If you remain in me.......

The latter part of John's Gospel contains a long discourse by Jesus as He seeks to prepare His disciples for His departure. In **John 15:7** He tells them that they can ask whatever they wish and get it as long as they remain in Him. Wow!

Our Part:

Remain in Jesus. The word translated remain has the deep meaning of remaining, dwelling in, enduring, waiting. We are called to make our relationship with Jesus our default position, the place which is our natural habitat, our home. This involves time, energy and intentionality. It also requires us to have His words remaining in us in the same way. This means spending time in the scriptures, meditating on Jesus' teaching and filling our mind with His purposes.

God's part:

He will do what we wish! Augustine's words come to mind here: 'Love God and live as you please.'

Implications:

Although when we properly remain in Jesus we will only ask for what honours Him what we are apt to forget is that He does want us to ask, that the Father likes to bless and the promise is meant to have actual, real outcome in our lives. It seems clear that answered prayer has a direct link with the depth of our relationship with Jesus. Sometimes we are so eager to demand that there are no first and second class Christians that we fail to realise what depth of relationship with the Lord is on offer.

We could go on with many other conditional promises (maybe in another book) but let this encourage you to find some yourself and think through the consequences for everyday living.

Chapter 9

How Do We Move Forward?

It is tempting to start with the reply to the apocryphal lost tourist in Ireland who when asking directions heard the words: 'If I were you I wouldn't start from here.'

However, here is where we are and how we get to where we need to be needs much thought and prayer. Since we began to write this book Brexit has happened and Donald Trump has been elected as President of the USA. Some people are in uproar about one or both of these happenings and everyone seems to be accusing others of peddling 'fake news'. Although the deliberate passing on of what is not true is a concern, it is slightly amusing to see the political and media classes so up in arms as in the past they had the monopoly of what news was passed on and therefore chose the 'fake news' themselves, otherwise known as propaganda. This was even before the rampant social media entered the fray thinking people were not certain what they could believe. Now the uncertainty is widespread except among those who only listen to people who agree with them!

It seems to us that the Christian church has fundamental choices to make and as those choices are made there is likely to be a major realignment of church groupings. We must choose whether or not we see scripture as our authority. We must choose whether or not we still believe the Gospel of salvation by grace through faith true and effectively life changing. We must choose whether to become absorbed into the prevailing views of society at any given time or seek to remain a people of a different Kingdom and different values.

We must choose to repent of ungodly living, of abuse of others, of abuse of God's word and much more. We must choose to seek God that we might again model to a dying world a radical alternative to the sense of hopelessness and dislocation that is out there. This alternative is rooted in obedience to what God has said.

It may be that for a time it seems as if this message is being lost in the crowded philosophies of a decaying world. However, there will come a day when either God will pour out His Spirit once more in revival and the mess we are allowing will be revealed for what it is, or He will decide the time has come for Jesus to return and then there will be judgment.

For now God is looking for Christians and church communities that will walk in obedience to His word, depend upon His Spirit and speak out lovingly yet with prophetic challenge to individuals, communities, governments and even other churches.

About The Authors

Stuart Woodward has been a Baptist Minister since 1982. He was, until recently Senior Minister at Kingswood Baptist Church, Basildon and is now Minister of Friars Baptist Church, Shoeburyness. He is married to Betty and also has two children (both active in church life) and five grandchildren.

Paul Woodward has been involved full time in the leadership of churches in the New Frontiers network since 1985. He is now retired having recently led Jubilee Church in Teesside. He is married to Jean, has two children (both active in church life) and five grandchildren.

Both Stuart and Paul were brought up in and came to faith through the Salvation Army. There are, however, significant differences. Paul is a natural engineer and loves to spend time with his model trains. Stuart loves sport, especially football and cricket and enjoys bird watching.

Both authors are passionate about Jesus, the Church and the Kingdom.

Printed in Great Britain
by Amazon